Not in the House!

Not in The House!

The Ultimate Guide to Potty Training Your Puppy

Brittany Boykin

Copyright © 2017 by Brittany Boykin

All rights reserved. No part of this publication may be reproduced, distributed, or transmitted in any form or by any means, including photocopying, recording, or other electronic or mechanical methods, without the prior written permission of the publisher, except in the case of brief quotations embodied in critical reviews and certain other noncommercial uses permitted by copyright law.

CAC Publishing

ISBN: 978-1-948489-25-6

Brittany Boykin

With all the dog food recalls lately, aren't you worried about what you're feeding your best friend? If you're interested in learning more about dog nutrition and homemade dog food and treat recipes, make sure to check out my other book titled 'Homemade Dog Treats and Homemade Dog Food.' You can grab it HERE!

Contents

- INTRODUCTION 10
- CHAPTER ONE 12
- What to Expect? 12
  - Indicators 16
  - Puppy or Adult Toilet Training - Is There a Difference? 17
  - Potty Training Tactics 18
  - Expectations for Puppyhood 19
- CHAPTER TWO 25
- Outdoor or Indoor Training? 25
  - Preparation is Crucial 25
  - Choosing Your Pup's Toilet Spot 27
  - Crate 29
  - Regular Schedule and Getting the Pup to the Potty Spot Quickly 31
  - How Often Should You Take Your Puppy Out? 33
- CHAPTER THREE 38
- Constant Supervision 38
  - Set Up a Routine 39
  - Supervise 41
  - Confinement 42
  - Housebreaking 43
  - Cue Words 44
  - How to Potty Train a Dog to Go in One Spot 45

Further Vital Information 47
CHAPTER FOUR 49
Eliminating Accidents 49
   Why Pups You Thought Were Housetrained Might Have Mishaps 50
   Some Other Reasons Your Puppy Might House Soil 51
   Recap - House Training Steps 54
   Additional Housetraining Tips 55
   What NOT to Do 56
   Tips and Reminders 57
CONCLUSION 61

INTRODUCTION

Before we even begin, you cannot assume that your puppy will be fully housetrained before he/she is six months old. Although most are, all breeds are different. Having said that, your puppy can be housetrained within 1 to 6 weeks. A good part of puppy potty training is determined by the puppy's size and breed, but also by the amount of effort you put into housetraining.

In reality, most puppies do not have sufficient bladder and bowel control before the age of 16 weeks. Meaning, most are unable to "hold it" for long periods of time. This also means that you will need to be extra attentive during this period. It is certainly advised that you begin housetraining as soon as you get your new puppy, but you must expect a handful of accidents. This is normal, and the purpose of this book is to give you all of the information you need to deal with these mishaps appropriately, from the proper way to react, to tips on cleaning up.

Puppy potty training is not always as simple as keeping

the dog on a regular eating, drinking and outdoor routine every few hours. And, as previously stated, you cannot expect your dog to be fully housetrained within a week or two.

Of course, there is a chance that you have an advanced puppy that this could happen with; however, many of them do continue to be only partially housetrained, or they have accidents for months. These smart puppies do comprehend that it's good to go potty outdoors, but they do not always understand that inside is not good. At the beginning, they might even come back inside after playtime or exercise and relieve themselves in the house.

Puppy toilet training is not simply about teaching them where to go. It is also about teaching them that other areas are unacceptable, until going only in the right spot becomes a habit.

CHAPTER ONE

What to Expect?

Below are some ways to predict when your dog needs to relieve him/herself:

- ✓ First thing in the morning (immediately after waking up)

- ✓ After each meal

- ✓ After drinking water

- ✓ After waking up from a nap

- ✓ During and/or after playing and exercising

- ✓ After gnawing on chew toys

- ✓ After any excitement

- ✓ After a ride in a vehicle

- ✓ After smelling another dog's urine or seeing them pee

- ✓ Upon leaving the crate

- ✓ Last thing at night (before sleep)

As you can clearly see, your dog will need to go out frequently at the start. Rest assured that this will end with some patience and time and, as he/she gets older, they will need to be taken out a lot less often.

Below is a guide that covers the predictability of trips to go potty needed day and night with regards to the age of your new puppy.

6-8 weeks - every 30 minutes (for toy and small breeds), 45 minutes (for medium breeds), 60 minutes (for large breeds) and 90 minutes (for giant breeds); with one or two trips during the night

8 to 12 weeks - every 2 hours, one trip during the night

12 to 16 weeks - every 2 hours; one trip for toy and small breeds during the night, none for other sizes

16 to 20 weeks - every 3 hours; none during the night

20 to 30 weeks - 4 to 5 times a day; none during the night

30+ weeks - 3 to 4 times a day; none during the night

12 months old - 3 times a day; none during the night

In addition, you should keep in mind that your puppy will most likely want to go to the bathroom anywhere between one and 30 minutes after eating and within 20 minutes of drinking a lot of water.

Clearly, these are general guidelines, but if you use a schedule, as above, your puppy's internal clock will have the capability of anticipating when to go. Because dogs learn by repetition, each time he/she goes in the proper place, they will be reinforced with good behavior.

Throughout the first week, the more trips to go potty, the better. It is best, if you can, to take some time off from work when you first bring your puppy home. By teaching good habits from the very first day, you will be better off in the long run and can spend the rest of your days enjoying your dog.

If you choose to take a week or so off from work, do your best not to have the puppy with you all the time. It may be hard, but you will not be there at all times when you return to work, and you will make it harder for the puppy to adjust when you are gone. Instead, follow a normal daily schedule. That way:

➢ You will speed up your puppy's housetraining development by bringing him outdoors or to his designated place indoors more often than you could if you had been working; and

➢ You will help your puppy recognize that being alone is not the end of the world.

There are actually two spots that your dog can eliminate: outdoors in the specified "elimination area" or indoors at his "potty paper." Perhaps the most common mistake new owners make is to think that paper training is the initial step to housetraining. It's actually not. Housetraining, or outdoor training, is the technique of training your puppy to eliminate outside all the time, while indoor training consists of training your dog to eliminate at an intended place inside your house.

Indicators

Most puppies will follow a routine prior to eliminating. Your job is to figure out how to "read" your pet. To assist you with this chore, listed below are the signs you should be conscious of:

✓ Your puppy whimpers

✓ His/her tail is rising

✓ He/she runs around in circles

- ✓ He/she sniffs raptly at the floor, carpet, or ground in search of the right spot

- ✓ He/she paces restlessly

- ✓ He/she scratches at the door

- ✓ He/she moves out of the playing area

- ✓ He/she squats

As soon as you observe any of these behaviors, stop what you are doing, put the leash on and take the puppy outside to the elimination zone or inside to the toilet stop. If your puppy begins peeing, interject by speaking a firm "outside" or "toilet" and then take him/her to the potty spot.

Puppy or Adult Toilet Training - Is There a Difference?

The housetraining method is the same for a puppy or an adult. The only difference is that an adult dog can hold it a lot longer than a puppy. Therefore, it might be easier to teach an adult dog. However, it can also be tricky because your adult dog comes with a history, and because of this, you won't always know how the previous owner trained him/her.

The crate training portion of the technique may take a bit longer with a grownup dog.

Potty Training Tactics

Prevention Is Key

The secret to effective potty training is taking your puppy out regularly (usually every 2 hours for an eight-week-old puppy) and never giving the puppy a chance to have an accident. This consists of approximately a minimum of at least 8 trips every day.

To prevent giving your puppy a chance to have an accident anywhere else in your house he/she should always either be:

- in the crate

- in a safe playpen with an area which has a good potty surface (such as pee pads)

- attached to a leash at your side so he/she cannot wander off to go potty

- under your nonstop supervision in an enclosed area. This means you are watching at all times.

If you follow this plan for at least a month straight, your puppy will consistently get into the habit of going outside and holding it inside. When this happens, continue keeping a close eye on him/her for another month or so, mainly when you take the pup on outings to other people's households, before confirming that he/she is totally potty trained.

Expectations for Puppyhood

Another crucial key to effective potty training is understanding your puppy. Below is a guide of what you can expect with regards to puppyhood:

When it comes to your puppy, their life is all about

"Me, Me, Me!" Assume nothing more than that. Essentially, in their minds, their "humans" are their servants at this stage. Their needs emulate the immediate needs of a baby or young toddler. Always remember that it has nothing to do with your puppy being a brat, they just don't know any better at this early stage and it's just his/her immediate needs that need tending to. Thus, tend to them instantly.

Lots of love, love, love. Because this is the phase of affection, you will effortlessly fall in love with your puppy. Therefore, be sure to take lots of pictures, but be careful not to overdo and spoil your puppy beyond repair. This will undoubtedly be the toughest part of raising your pup, but is extremely important in creating a cooperative, good dog.

While you will discover vital skills that you can begin to generate during the puppy's younger stages, you are pretty much in a "stand still" of sorts. Your puppy is simply too young for appropriate obedience training at this life stage. Your mission now is to stop errors, instill concepts, and keep your puppy safe until he/she can learn obedience skills.

Puppies act on instinct. They come equipped with only their dog dispositions and are acting strictly on what they know inherently. They are not in charge of their emotions, nor do they pre-plan their actions. They simply act on their instincts until their "humans" teach them to withstand impulses. Do not punish, but rather redirect them, and always stay patient!

Boundaries: Puppies factually have no self-control during this period. They commonly do whatever pops up in their tiny minds. This is part predisposition and part lack of self-control. Do not assume your puppy will make good choices or constantly be well behaved.

Attempting to stop your puppy's instinctual behaviors won't work. You can teach your puppy to stop using his/her mouth to converse when you teach him/her a different method of communicating, but, until then, attempting to use "quick fixes" to detain these behaviors will only lessen your puppy's self-assurance in you as their leader.

Puppies have restricted attention spans and can only "be good," or in other words, be kept out of trouble, for a limited period of time. As they grow older, and as their owners train them, they will cultivate a much better attention span. It is important that you understand now, however, that they can only focus for short periods of time.

When the puppy's mental battery has reduced and is monotonous, that is when improper behaviors begin, and any attempt to refocus will pretty much become useless. You may want to, at this point, take your puppy to their crate for a rest.

Keep in mind that at this young age, your puppy can learn the housebreaking routine, but his/her body cannot hold all of their bodily functions notwithstanding how much they may want to. At approximately 4 ½ to 5 months of age, your puppy's body will begin to develop and that is when they begin to control the flow of pee from the body. Very regular potty breaks will aid in it's routine.

Have sensible expectations of your puppy. Puppyhood is the stage where owners are the ones who are completely responsible for their new little bundles of joy. Do not assume that your puppy will perform like an adult dog. Know his/her limits and work with them into the next stage of learning.

CHAPTER TWO

Outdoor or Indoor Training?

Depending upon your situation, you will be required to decide if you are going to train your puppy to eliminate outside or inside your home. It is strongly recommended to train the puppy to go outside if you have a yard or close access to a park or street.

If you are living in a high-rise apartment, or if you have a disability, it can be hard to train your dog to go outside. Therefore, indoor training in a particular portion of the house is suggested.

Likewise, owners of a toy breed who live in a region where it is cold in the winter may also choose to train their dogs inside.

Preparation is Crucial

It is best to have everything prepared and ready prior to your puppy's arrival. However, if you already have your dog, this chapter will simply help you recall what to do.

During the course of the training process, there are two types of confinement:
- Short-term
- Long-term

In order to confine your puppy for short periods of time, use the crate.

When you need to leave your puppy for more than a couple of hours, you will need to use long-term confinement. The best thing to do is to block off a portion of a room in your house you are fine with your pup having access to. You can use a gate to implement this effectively.

In your puppy's own special little area (such as the crate or a small den), be sure to fill it with chew toys. It is also a good idea to place a plastic sheet under the paper in order to protect your floors. This place is your puppy's domain, thus everyone in the household must be aware of and respect it.

According to experts, the best part of the house to put the den/crate is near your kitchen. The kitchen is generally the best choice because it is frequently the busiest place in the house. Puppies really need to feel that they are part of the family and being in the center of the action is very encouraging for them. And, in general, a kitchen floor is easier to clean than a carpet or wood floor.

To block off parts of the room, as mentioned above, you can use baby gates. They are simple to install and open when it is time to take your puppy out. You may also use a playpen to confine your dog. Most pet stores have them, but they can be a bit pricier.

Your puppy's very own special place, or domain, should be restricted with gates or boards, and his/her crate should be put in a corner. The floor should be covered with old bed sheets or brown paper (which is better than newspaper).

Choosing Your Pup's Toilet Spot

You need to choose the spot that you want your puppy

to eliminate. For those who will be outdoor training your puppy, select a spot that is easily available and fairly quiet and that will not get too muddy. For example, pick a corner in your back yard that isn't too close to the street, that way your pup won't get preoccupied when it is time for him/her to do their business.

Clearly, for city pups, the elimination spot will most likely be the gutter. Nonetheless, no matter which spot you choose, it is essential that you train your pup to be comfortable in it. Actually, this is not a hard thing to achieve as dogs have an enormously powerful sense of smell. It really only takes one urination and elimination for your dog to distinguish the spot after. The smell of his/her own pee and poop will activate your pup's need to eliminate and will speed-up the entire process.

Dogs have this instinct to want to refresh their own spot, simply to mark it and for other dogs to not claim the spot for their own. In this aspect, dogs are very territorial.

The toilet stop is the same as the elimination zone except it is inside the house. You need to decide on a spot that won't be in the way, but also not too out-of-the-way that your puppy will have a hard time finding it. Experts typically recommend the bathroom. The floor surface is generally easy to clean up and there is usually a product close by that makes it easier to get rid of the odor.

Training begins with your puppy learning to love to be in and sleep in their crate, or other enclosed area.

The purpose of crate training is for your puppy to learn to love resting in the crate and recognize it as its den. Dogs love to have a den.

Crate

Your puppy should be sleeping in the crate at night and taking naps in it during the day. In order to train him/her to love the crate, you can make it comfortable with a blanket and put treats inside at random times. Then, give the pup toys and pet him/her when he/she gets in it before closing the door. The ultimate objective of crate training is where your dog will go into the crate on its own or when you give a spoken prompt, as opposed to requiring him/her to be thrust or persuaded in. In addition, once the dog is in, he/she is stress-free, comfy and quiet.

Crate Size

The crate you purchase should be large enough for your puppy to grow into. When inside, they should have enough room to turn around and lie down. However, you do not want it to be big enough for the dog to have enough room for a potty area. You can buy a divider at the pet store to make your puppy's crate a bit smaller and, when your puppy begins to grow, you can make the crate bigger by moving or removing the divider.

Most puppies will whimper the first time they are crated. This is because they are not used to having limited access to their humans. Puppies must learn early on that being apart from their family for short periods of time, or that being restricted to a small space, is okay. This way, when you have to leave, they will not be afraid. No matter how hard it may be, keep in mind that if you "stick to your guns" with regards to crate training in the early stages, the whimpering should stop or slow down quickly, usually within a week.

Remember that if you let the dog out when he/she whines, it becomes a reward to them and the whining could then become severe anxiety or an obstacle which prevents you from leaving your dog alone in another room or at home when you go out.

Regular Schedule and Getting the Pup to the Potty Spot Quickly

First Thing in the Morning

When you let the puppy out of his/her crate, be quick to get the pup outside before it has a chance to go to the bathroom in the house. If you are not sure that the puppy can hold it long enough to make it outside, carry him/her out to the spot. They will not pee on you.

Rush Out to the Potty Spot

When taking the puppy out, walk quickly or run so he/she does not have the opportunity to get distracted or stop. Initially, the puppy might have to be on a leash so he/she does not even have the chance to stop. Even a one-second stop will give the pup a chance to squat and go inside. Therefore, if you have stairs, it would be better to carry the puppy, simply because its hesitancy right before the first stair is enough to permit the pup to squat and pee.

Stand Around Until He/She Goes Potty

Once you are outside, keep the dog on a leash so it doesn't have the chance to wander around and get distracted, or else put him/her in a small restricted area outside. Stand there with the pup silently until he/she goes potty. When that happens, praise, pet or give a treat right after finishing. This will reinforce that he/she has done a good thing. Just be careful not to distract the pup from finishing. If after 5 or so minutes the pup doesn't go potty, put it in the crate for approximately 15 minutes and then repeat the process.

Do this until he/she goes potty outside. After that, you can play with your pup, but not until then.

Yes, it can be tedious initially, but it will be well worth it in the end when the pup is fully trained. You may want to listen to music or a book on tape while you wait for the pup to go, and you may also want to consider using a timer so you don't get impatient for the 5 minutes outside.

How Often Should You Take Your Puppy Out?

Begin with every 2 hours for an eight-week-old puppy. In addition, eight-week-old puppies can be crated for up to 2 hours in the daytime and 2-4 hours at night while they sleep. During the day, your puppy can be in its crate for about the same number of hours as they are old in months. So, let's say you have a 2-month-old puppy, you can crate for 2 hours at a time, if the puppy has not had a lot of water prior to going in.

Take the Puppy Out After a Nap

Take the puppy out immediately upon waking or as soon as they are let out of their playpen or crate.

Take the Puppy Out After a Play Session

If your puppy doesn't go, you can put him/her into the crate for 15 to 30 minutes and then take it out again.

Take the Puppy Out When its Body Language Shows it is Hunting for a Place to Go

Signs that the pup is about to go typically consist of them sniffing the ground, circling, or wandering away.

After a Drink

Take the puppy outside 10 to 20 minutes after it has had a drink of water. Eliminate the water about an hour before taking the pup out for the final potty trip of the day, so it can learn to go through the night without going potty. Your pup will eventually learn to go through the night for 7 to 8 hours.

Learn From Your Mistakes

Puppies initially will seem to have to go a hundred times a day. Learn along the way how to anticipate when your pup will need to go, and anticipate accidents. Every time your pup has an accident, you will learn from the experience and be able to avoid making the same mistakes.

With the correct potty training, you are creating the habit of your dog going to a potty spot whenever they have to go, never giving him/her the chance to have an accident inside.

Adding the Cue to Go Potty

When you are capable of consistently predicting when your puppy has to go, you can now add a cue word.

You will want to add the words "go potty" in a light voice only once, right before you think the dog is going to go to the bathroom. If you do this consistently, he/she will come to learn that "go potty" means he should do his business outside or in the toilet spot. Do not say the cue words over and over, or they will just turn into noise to the pup.

CHAPTER THREE

Constant Supervision

Until your pup is trained and reliable, he/she should be monitored at all times or close to you connected to a hands-free leash or near you on leash or in a playpen. He/she can also be outdoors in a safe area. This can be helpful so the puppy can go potty when you're not outside to watch over him/her. But then again, be sure to avoid leaving your puppy outside without supervision for hours at a time. Also, be sure to watch the weather as young puppies are less capable of withstanding too warm or too cold conditions.

Housetraining your puppy will require much more than a few piles of old newspapers - it requires attentiveness, tolerance, a good amount of commitment and most importantly, reliability.

Take a look at the methods below to assist in minimizing accidents.

All dogs, especially puppies, have accidents in the

house, and, probably, quite a lot. You must expect this when considering getting a puppy - it's part of living with the new little baby.

The more vigilant you are in following these procedures, the faster your dog will learn. It sometimes takes a few weeks to housetrain the pup, and with some of the smaller breeds, it could be longer.

Set Up a Routine

Just like babies, puppies will do their best when placed on a regular schedule. This routine teaches the pup that there are certain times to eat, play, and potty.

As stated previously, a puppy's bladder is small and they can only hold it for about one hour for every month of age. If you wait longer than this between potty breaks, you pup is certain to have an accident. So, if you work outside of your home, you will need to get assistance, such as asking a housemate (or family member) to help, or hire a dog walker.

And again, it is important to take your pup outside

often, approximately every 2 hours, and as soon as he/she wakes, while you are playing and after, and, of course, immediately after eating/drinking.

Choose a specific spot outside, and always got to that same spot using a leash. Reminder, while your pup is going to the bathroom, use your cue word or phrase, such as "go potty," and eventually you will only need to use this cue phrase or word to remind him/her to do their business.

And be sure to reward your pup every time they go to reiterate that they have done something good. Dogs will do anything for praise and rewards. Compliment him/her or give a treat, but be sure to do it immediately upon finishing and not after you get back inside the house. This step is important, because rewarding them for doing a good thing is the way they will know what's expected of them.

Keep your puppy on a regular feeding schedule. If kept on a regular eating schedule, they will only be on a regular eliminating schedule, making it easier to judge when they have to go out. Based on their age, puppies typically should be fed 3 to 4 times a day. Feeding your pup at the same times every day will make housetraining simpler for both of you.

Remove the puppy's water dish approximately 2 ½ hours prior to going to bed to lessen the chance that the pup will need to go potty during the nighttime. And, most puppies can sleep for around 7 hours without needing to go poop.

If your puppy does wake during the night, make sure you don't make a big issue of it. If you do, they will believe that it is playtime and won't go back to sleep. Keep it as dark as you can in the house, don't talk to or fool around with your puppy, take it outside, and bring the pup right back to bed.

Supervise

Do your best not to give the pup an opportunity to soil in the house. Keep close track of him/her whenever indoors.

It is best, until they are trained, to tie your puppy

somewhere close to you on a piece of furniture with a long leash if you aren't actively training or playing with the puppy. And, watch for the signs indicated earlier that your pup needs to eliminate. When you notice these signs, swiftly grab the leash and take the pup outside to its spot. Once the pup goes, pat and reward generously. They will want to please you quickly upon learning they will be praised.

Give your dog more freedom in the house and yard once they are reliably housetrained.

Confinement

You will not always be able to watch your pup 24/7. When you cannot, make sure he/she is in a limited area, small enough that they won't want to go to the bathroom in it. The area should, though, be large enough for them to comfortably stand, lie down, and turn around in, and that is all. It is recommended to use a portion of your bathroom or laundry room closed off with a baby gate.

The other alternative is to crate train your pup and use

the crate to confine them when you are not around. Just be sure not to leave them alone in the crate for an unreasonable amount of time. If your dog has spent more than a couple of hours in the crate, you will have to take them straight outside or to his/her toilet spot immediately upon letting them out, and, of course, remember to praise and reward.

Housebreaking
Establish a Routine

The first step to housebreaking your puppy is to establish a schedule. It is very crucial to stay as close to the same times every day until your dog has fully grasped the fact that you are training. The better you adhere to the schedule, the faster your puppy will create a timetable of their own.

Develop your schedule around the rhythms of your household. Begin when the household wakes, and take the pup for an immediate toilet break.

Write this schedule down, if necessary, and post it in a visible place in the house (like the refrigerator door).

If more than a few individuals will be taking care of the puppy, make sure that schedule duties are understood and followed by all. A united household will guarantee the success of your housebreaking endeavor.

Cue Words
Direction Cue

When walking towards the door, use a word such as "outside" to direct your puppy to the first part of the task. The cue "Outside" will let them know where you are going, and then by using the succeeding cue word for elimination once you get outside, the puppy will link the two words with the whole process.

"Outside" will be the question you will ask later if you think the pup may need to go outside. Once you have effectively connected "outside" with, say, "go potty", he/she will quickly run to the door in response to your question if they need to go.

Elimination Cue

You can use another cue work, such as "hurry" to propose that you wish the puppy to eliminate. This word can be associated simply with the first potty break of the morning.

Cue words are meant to be mild coaxes when your pup is becoming distracted in the yard. Repeat the cue "hurry" in a persuading voice and they will learn to refocus.

Some people choose to select one cue word for peeing and another for pooping. You need to use these cue words with the action quite a few times so your pup can make to distinction between the action and the words.

How to Potty Train a Dog to Go in One Spot

Without specific direction, dogs will create a mess of your yard when they relieve themselves anyplace they want. To avoid this, it is advantageous to train them to relieve themselves only in one specific area, and here is how you can do it:

Choose a Spot

Choose a spot which is away from the high-traffic areas of your yard. The spot you choose should be suitable for the size of your dog. A small area is fine for a small breed, but larger breeds will obviously require more room.

Sometimes dogs pick their own spot. If that is what your dog does, if at all possible, make this his/her spot.

Keep the Area Clean

You must be sure to keep your dog's area clean. You can, however, leave one pile in the area throughout training simply to remind your pet that it is the correct spot, but be sure not to leave any more than that. If the area becomes too messy and soiled, your dog might decide to find another place to relieve themselves.

Further Vital Information

It is extremely important, and just plain good manners, to always clean up after your dog. This is predominantly important if your dog eliminates on the street or in the park (this is especially true to people living in high-rise buildings or condominiums). Every time your dog poops, make sure that you dispose his waste properly. Make it a habit to bring a poop scoop and plastic or brown bag whenever you play with him around the neighborhood.

CHAPTER FOUR

Eliminating Accidents

Puppies need to know that it is not okay to pee and poop just anywhere. Potty training is a forthright process, but one that needs to be implemented positively (with no punishment that will scare your puppy) and dependably, following two basic rules:

- ✓ Avoiding indoor accidents by confinement and close monitoring, and

- ✓ Taking the puppy outside on a regular basis and rewarding him/her for eliminating where you want.

Accidents in the house will more than likely happen in many places within your home, but at times you will find that the puppy goes in a selected place, such as rarely used rooms or on a precise type of surface. Very young pups, under 12 weeks, do not yet have full bladder control and won't be able to hold it for long. Older puppies that have accidents are probably just not house trained completely.

Why Pups You Thought Were Housetrained Might Have Mishaps

Too Young to Be Fully House Trained

Some puppies, mainly those under 12 weeks, have not yet developed bladder or bowel control.

Incomplete Housetraining

Many puppies just have yet to learn where to go or they have yet to learn a means to tell their human when they need to go out. Some puppies will only have an accident in the house under certain conditions. For example, a puppy may have an accident when it has been home alone for a long period of time, sometimes very first thing in the morning or during the night while we sleep. Some other pups may pee or poop whenever they feel the necessity to go. For the most part, though, this is just incomplete housetraining.

Breakdown in Housetraining

There are times when pups seem to be house trained and at some point regress and start going in the house again.

There are some reasons for this:

Some Other Reasons Your Puppy Might House Soil

Urine Marking

If your puppy is over 3 months of age and pees slight amounts on vertical surfaces, it could be urine marking. Young dogs performing this behavior often elevate their hind legs when peeing.

Dogs are territorial. Urine marking is when they want to say "this is my spot," and they tell other individuals and animals by marking it. Sometimes your dog will bark first to warn potential trespassers that they are about to intrude on his/her grounds. The dog will then take it to the next level by urinating in a certain spot.

Separation Anxiety

If your pup only goes to the bathroom when left alone at home, even for a short time, it might have separation anxiety. You will notice that he/she appears anxious or upset right before you leave.

Submissive/Excitement Urination

Your pup may have a submissive/excitement urination dilemma if he/she only urinates during greetings, play/fun time, and physical contact. You might notice that the puppy displays submissive positions during interaction with you. He/she might flinch or shy away, roll over on belly, tuck or lower tail, duck head, avert eyes, flatten ears or all of the above.

Medical Reasons for House Soiling

You should always consult your puppy's vet to eliminate any medical causes for house soiling. Some prevalent medical reasons for untimely urination and defecation are:

Urinary Tract Infection

Puppies will, at times, come down with a UTI and they will have to pee often in tiny amounts. Be patient with your puppy always. In addition, they might lick their genitals more than usual.

Intestinal Upset

If your puppy has already been trained to go to the bathroom outside and has begun to have a bowel movement of loose stools or diarrhea, he/she might have intestinal upset.

Change in Diet

If you have just recently changed the kind of food your puppy eats, that could potentially be the issue. More often than not, after a diet change, this will happen. The puppy will most likely need to poop more frequently or on a different schedule than before the change.

Recap - House Training Steps

- Keep your puppy on a consistent daily feeding schedule.

- Take your puppy outside regularly.

- In between, know where your puppy is at all times. Watch for early signs that the puppy needs to pee and/or poop so that you can anticipate and prevent accidents.

- If you are unable to keep an eye on your puppy, it should be limited to a small room or crate. If leaving in a room, be sure to either leave the door closed or block the doorway with a gate. Otherwise, you can tether the puppy to you with a leash which won't give it much freedom around you. Progressively give your puppy more freedom – in a small area, and little by little increasing it to larger areas, or multiple rooms, in your home.

- Be sure to stay outside with your puppy and

give lots of loving, hugs/kisses, treats, play.

- If you catch your puppy in the act of going in the house, clap sharply twice, adequate enough to startle but not scare it. When startled, the dog will normally stop mid-stream. Quickly run the pup in a motivating way. Never punish. Allow your pet to finish outside, and then reward with happy praise and a small treat.

Additional Housetraining Tips

- Clean accidents with an enzymatic cleanser to lessen odors that might lure the puppy back to the same spot.

- Just because your dog is housetrained in your home, he may still have accidents when in another person's home. You should try to monitor your puppy carefully when you visit new places and be sure to take him/her out often.

What NOT to Do

- Do not ever rub your pup's nose in its pee or poo.

- Do not reprimand your pet for having an accident in the house. If you catch him/her going to the bathroom inside, make a startling noise for the pup to hear. Then immediately take your puppy outside and show where it "the spot", wait until he/she finishes, and then give praise.

- Never physically punish your puppy for accidents. Know that if your pup has accidents in the house, you neglected to properly supervise it.

- Do not clean with ammonia-based products. Urine contains ammonia. Cleaning with ammonia can attract your puppy back to the same spot to pee again.

Tips and Reminders

1. If your housetraining relapses, back up a week or two in the process and start over.

2. If your new bundle of joy has a lot of diarrhea, always be aware that it could be very sick. Puppies can become dehydrated to a fatal degree very fast. The wisest thing to do in this situation is to be "safe" and not "sorry." You should call your puppy's veterinarian right away.

3. If you have a paper-trained puppy and they will not go to the bathroom on anything other than paper, take a bit of newspaper or a pee pad outside and have them go on it. Each ensuing trip, decrease the size of the paper or pad until it is gone.

4. If your dog has decided to soil its den, you may have to remove the bedding from the crate. Try the bare crate floor, and set an alarm clock to wake you up at intermittent times during the night so that you can check on your pup and take it out when needed.

5. Neutering a male dog between the ages of 8 weeks and 6 months will lessen the development of territorial leg-lifting.

6. If your veterinarian ever puts your dog on a steroid called Prednisone, be aware that it can cause your dog to want to drink much more than usual, which, in turn, will cause them to urinate much more.

7. A lot of exercise can also make your dog drink more water and urinate more.

8. When your little cutie has been trained to go to the bathroom on cue, you may want to teach him/her to poop and pee on other surfaces, such as cement, gravel, dirt, grass, etc. Dogs, for the most part, have their own preference, such as grass, and might refuse to go on anything but their preferred surface. Hence, if you are ever in a setting where there is no grass, you and your dog could be in trouble.

9. Lastly, if your circumstances do not permit you to be at home more and your puppy is always waiting to go for longer periods than is realistic, do not be afraid to consider training your dog with a litter box. Many

people do this, especially those who live in apartments.

CONCLUSION

Housetraining your puppy calls for much more than a few piles of old newspaper. It requires patience, caution, persistence, plenty of commitment and most importantly, consistency.

The better you are in following the above housetraining suggestions, the quicker the pup or adult dog will learn. It will take a little time and patience, but when you succeed, and you will, it will be something you and your dog will benefit from for years to come.

I cannot stress enough, when housetraining, it is extremely important to create a routine. Just like infants, puppies function best on a regular routine. This routine teaches the puppy that there is a time and place for everything: eat, play, nap, and potty.

Lastly, don't expect your dog to be perfect.

If you enjoyed this book and picked up some awesome potty training tips, I would be sincerely grateful if you could leave a review on Amazon. Reviews are the best way to help your fellow readers sort through the nonsense so make sure to help them out! Leave A Review

With all the dog food recalls lately, aren't you worried about what you're feeding your best friend? If you're interested in learning more about dog nutrition and homemade dog food and treat recipes, make sure to check out my other book titled 'Homemade Dog Treats and Homemade Dog Food.' You can grab it HERE!

www.ingramcontent.com/pod-product-compliance
Lightning Source LLC
Chambersburg PA
CBHW021159080526
44588CB00008B/410